Growing Pains

No rain, no flowers.

Growing Pains

a collection of poetry and prose

—

Alexandra Rain

alexandra@growingpainsbyrain.com
growingpainsbyrain@gmail.com
Published in the United States by
Kindle Direct Publishing (KDP)
Cover design by Anna Grayson
Edited by Tiffany Grayson

For Zoe.

There are no villains in this story. Just real people.

Introduction

I've called the police on my parents twice in my life. The first time, I was seven. The second time, I was eighteen. The call at age seven was a result of my father and me playing games. It was nothing serious. He was messing around and pretending to be dead – not enough to scare me but enough to give me a laugh.

I suppose I got annoyed at his jokes at some point and I called 911, trying to give him a scare back. I put the home phone on speaker so he could hear it ring, and immediately hung up. Still, the police showed up at our apartment. I hid in my room, embarrassed. My father eventually got me out of my room and the police examined my arms and legs (checking for bruises, my father explained afterward).

Everything was fine.

The second time I called the police, everything was not fine. I was calling to report, as stolen, the items my mother had taken. This was not the first time she had gone through the house and decided what might be of value to feed her addiction, and I was certain it was not going to be the last.

Eleven years passed between the time of the first call and the second. This is the account of what happened during that time.

Blue Childhood

My childhood was blue.

My childhood was watching the snowstorms cover the blue skies
  in January,

Staining my hands with blue-ink pens in February,

Zipping up my navy jacket in March.

My childhood was watching April showers,

Covering my entire sidewalk with chalk in the May heat,

Blowing out blue birthday candles in June.

My childhood was swimming pools in the middle of July,

Forgetting to put on sunscreen in August,

Dancing and spinning until I was completely dizzy in September.

My childhood was unwrapping blue pieces of candy in October,

Staring at constellations in cold November air,

And the darkest days in December.

Throughout the years, my childhood was the slamming of doors and

the crashing of voices, eavesdropping on grown-up conversations,

trying to stitch the pieces together.

My childhood was forgiving again and again, and faking a brave
  face.

My childhood was blue.

Nine

You promised me everything would be fine.

You sat me on your bed, spoke words of comfort, swearing I did
  nothing wrong.

And yet.

You and I both knew change was near.

Holding back tears, you said, "I love you, my dear."

And even though care was there, the pounding stayed in my head.

Divorce

I knew from the look in my mother's eyes.

On that day, her eyes were a shade duller than usual and coated over
with a look that was not quite disappointment, but almost.

Something in her eyes told me, and before she opened her mouth, I
already knew the truth.

Character Development

Amidst all the yells, the character I built for him fell.

He was not as charming as I had once believed.

In the pools of problems, the great man I thought I knew had
  begun to leave.

Kid Again

I was the child, yet the kid in you was beginning to show.

Not in an adventurous, wonderful way; there was no wonder in your
eyes.

You appeared little.

Every movement timid, every word unsure.

All I wanted to do was find you a cure.

Divorce, Again

I watched my parents' love grow cold.

And then warm again.

And then cold again.

Warm again, cold again, warm again, cold again.

It was a never-ending cycle.

I wondered how it was possible that love and hate could be so
easily transposed.

Day Dreams of Flight

We continued as best as we could.

Acting normal, like we believed we should.

Behind the mask of an average face,

I stared at the birds moving at their own pace.

I admired the way the birds took flight.

I wanted to fly, but all I could manage was to cry.

And so, because I was a girl with arms instead of wings,

I sat and listened as everyone told me it would be alright.

Truly, I tried,

To believe their words with all of my might.

Zoe

I never took flight.

Soon, the racing birds left my sight.

Just as they passed, so did the light.

It was at night that my parents began to fight.

It all felt cold.

The slamming of doors, the crashing of screams.

I only had her little hand to hold.

She was only two.

Her eyes weren't quite blue;

Rather, they were the richest shade of brown.

Amidst all of the yelling, she would frown.

This little girl, with a head full of curls,

And a heart that was sweet and kind,

Made me change my mind.

How could I dare think of flying, when my little sister was crying?

Ten

The fridge was nearly empty.

I looked into my older sister's dark eyes, and asked,

"Have their money problems gotten worse?"

She shrugged, sheepishly, saying, "I don't know."

The shrug was all I needed. The lack of confidence in her answer

made it very clear that things certainly were not getting better.

Divorce, Again and Again

The pattern continued, like a flickering light switch.

One day on, the next day off.

One month, they would try.

The next month, they were giving up.

At some point, I gave up too.

I stopped trying to keep track of the scoreboard.

I lost my interest in whether love or hate was in the lead.

Broken Promise

I was crying.

The reason why has left my mind.

However, some details remain the same.

The smell of your grey T-shirt, the freckles scattered over your arms.

The way you looked me directly in the eyes and said, "I love you."

You tucked my hair behind my ear, trying to hide your own fears.

Your voice cracked as you promised,

"It is all going to be okay. This will be over soon."

And yet,

The pain stayed even with the changing of the moon.

Eleven

Your eyes were nearly dim.

Your sentences were not precise or clear.

Every time I was near enough to hear,

You sounded senseless.

Despite this, I knew you still cared.

But I could not ignore that parts of you were leaving.

You did not have the light you once did;

I remember seeing it as a kid.

But I was eleven now, and it was my turn to be brave.

With all of the courage I could find, I said,

"Don't worry, Mum, it'll be fine."

Sun-Day

I remember the way the sun felt that day.

I could feel the sun's warmth cover every bare part of my skin.

The sun reached the back of my neck, the tops of my hands, and the
  parts of my cheeks into which my smile stretched.

Everything was bright. I was happy, I mean, extremely happy.

The pure bliss of innocent childhood.

I had laughed so hard my ribs had started going tough.

I remember the way I felt like the sun that day.

And then the phone rang.

I answered and, suddenly, my heart dropped.

It sunk to the very bottoms of my feet.

I heard my mother speak on the other end, shakily.

Her words could not make their way through her sobs.

She asked for my grandmother, who was within arm's-length reach.

I passed my grandmother the phone.

I listened as yet another adult promised it would be fine.

This time the promise was not directed to me; the promise was
  intended for my mother, who clearly was not fine.

And then the details begin to blur.

I remember watching my mother cry in complete misery on our
  bathroom floor.

I remember the adults avoiding conversation with me.

I was left with no explanation.

I remember visiting my mother in a rehabilitation center, a few
weeks after the call.

But mostly, I remember the way the sun felt that day.

Misplaced Blame

He is a hurricane.

And when the storm is finished,

He makes you feel the guilt for it,

As if *you* were responsible for the disaster.

Kitchen Floor

In a drunken state, he had grabbed all of his clothes.

He did not bother to put them in boxes – there was an urgency in his
movement.

He grabbed the clothes as they were, on their hangers, and tossed
them into his car.

The air rang with his anger;

His words were devils dancing into my ears.

I had never witnessed anyone in such a rage as I did with my
father in that moment.

Before I had the courage to find my voice, he was gone.

He had stormed out, leaving a mess of confusion

And a disaster of a daughter.

By the innocence of my young mind, I expected not to see him again.

Ever.

The next morning, he called, announcing his return.

I burst into panic.

I was choking, yet there were no hands around my neck.

I could not breathe – the rising and falling of my chest had
quickened to an unnatural speed.

And quite suddenly, everything became unreal.

I screamed, like a wolf howling at the moon, to the alarm of my little
sister.

I shook, my trembling hands reaching to my head.

I wanted to pull every piece of my hair out.

I lost control.

Every inch of my being was in pain.

The kitchen floor had turned into spikes.

My father had turned into a monster.

Love Him, Love Him Not

Do I love him?

Do I hate him?

I can never settle any real feeling except for the lack of attachment.

Your coldness finds me on even the warmest of days.

Consequence of Reality

You are the kind of person who is adored from a distance.

Strangers admire you, but when they get close enough to see your
reality,

Disappointment strikes.

Peace Maker

My role in life has been to hold everyone's hands, put on a brave
face, and, with my strongest voice, tell them,
"Don't worry, it will be okay."

The trouble with fulfilling this role is that, when everyone is away,
I can't tell myself, "Don't worry, it will be okay," without my voice
cracking.

Phobia of Self

I have to remind myself I should not fear my emotions.

I should not be scared of my own beating heart or the trembling of
my hands.

I should not be ashamed of the tears rolling down my cheeks.

I should not fear my ability to feel so deeply.

New Home

My parents, little sister, and I moved into my grandparents' house by the start of my freshman year in high school. The move was easy for me. Their house already felt like home. My mother, sister Zoe, and I had moved in and out a few times already as my parents navigated their on-and-off relationship.

My grandparents had always been my best friends. If I ever needed refuge, I knew I could call them. They had only ever treated me with welcome arms. Within the walls of their home, I felt peace.

For my parents, the feeling of moving must have felt something different. My mind was too young to understand the weight that comes with moving back in' home in your mid-30s.
The shame my mother felt slipped out through her mouth occasionally. If I had been paying more attention, I would have noticed her embarrassment. But at age 14, my mind was focused on superficial matters. My attention could not have been further away from my mother's feelings. I regret that now more than ever.

I was relieved to be out of our old house. I felt as though the new address I had would allow me to fit in. I was horribly selfish.

La Lune

She was like the moon.

She was always there, like how the moon hangs in the night sky.

Sometimes she was more apparent than others, her figure clearly
   shown.

Other times, she disappeared, although never completely.

There was a presence of her that I could feel.

She controlled me, much like the moon controls the tides.

For years, I watched her and grew fascinated with her complicated
   nature.

I found myself encompassed in a tide of her own.

In the early years, I floated easily.

She had a light in her eyes, a warmth in her touch. She smiled often.

As I aged, she changed. Her smile showed more sporadically.

Her eyes remained bright but they rested under eyebrows that were
   constantly stitched together by the string of stress.

Try as she might, her worries couldn't hide.

I curiously watched her struggle.

I wondered whether it was the financial troubles or the attempted
   separation from an alcoholic husband that caused her anxiety.

I desperately swam against the brutality of her tides.

She ended up in a hospital.

I was eleven then.

Fear overtook me.

My terror transformed into a twisted wonder.

Standing between those white walls, where the silence was horribly sharp, I asked myself, "How did she end up here?"

Much like the moon, she remained a mystery.

The only sense of certainty was the moment she promised, "I love you. It will be okay."

But even then, her touch was cooling and her eyes were turning dull.

Afterwards, she wasn't the same. Her voice was no longer sweet as honey.

She tried to speak smoothly but whenever she opened her mouth, the words came out through cracks.

I wondered whether it was the exhaustion or just her depression that caused her behavior.

She lost her job. She started disappearing, never returning at the hour she'd promised.

Her touch became frozen, her smile vanished.

She lost her kind nature, turning easily mean.

Between all of our intense disagreements and the exposure of her addictions, our love thinned.

Her ocean was unbearable; I drowned under her vicious waves. With each passing month, my heart continued to break.

Even still, I remained horribly captivated, ever so fascinated by my mother.

Eight O' One - Eight Five Six - Eight Nine Five One

I had your number memorized since the first grade.

You were always in reach.

Then your number began changing, at an alarming rate.

I couldn't keep up with the change, my legs were sore from all the
  chasing.

And just like that, you were out of reach.

Candor

I want to write beautifully and wonderfully.

I want my words to be poetic, but no amount of poetry or clever
rhymes can cover the truth. The truth is harsh and ugly, and trying
to write "beautifully" won't fix that. Trying to write "wonderfully"
won't heal me. So I must write honestly.

The truth is, I can't remember whether it was a Monday or a Tues-
day. I just remember it was a weeknight. I had just finished dance
and I was waiting for my mum. Again. She was an hour late. I had
homework piled up at home, which surely contributed to my
irritability. When I got in the car and saw him, her mysterious friend,
a nerve ticked. I had exceeded past the point of impatience.

As per usual, my mum acted like everything was fine and that all
was normal. She babbled on, giving a poor excuse as to why she was
so late. She was generously helping a friend move. The excuse
continued past reason. When I realized all logic was lost, I also realized I was not my mother's first choice. Her friend had taken over
that spot. This only proved more clear when we returned home to
find my little nine-year-old sister entirely alone. I felt the pain of her
abandonment deeper than I felt my own. I don't want to imagine
how long she was alone while our mother had disappeared.

In the absence of my grandparents, there was no one there to protect her or me. I do not know if I've ever felt so alone.

Naturally, I phoned my grandparents, who happened to be visiting their other daughter in California. Sitting on the back porch (as far away from my mother as I could be), I cried. In the release of emotions, I told them all of what had happened. To my mother, I must have appeared to be reporting. And perhaps I was. My intention with the phone call was not to make her look bad; I just wanted to find some peace in the cold of night. And, though I tried to hide, my mother found me. The last words I heard my grandmother say before the phone got snatched away was, "Don't let her bully you."

My mother dragged me inside. Truthfully, I can't remember whether she had hold of my shirt of wrist. I remember how her grasp was horribly tight and harsh. In that very moment, my sweet mother had been replaced with someone foreign to me. Every inch she stepped closer to me, I flinched. I was convinced she was going to hit me. Her hold on me may have left a few marks but she did not strike me. She didn't need to. The way she yelled at me inflicted enough pain.

I should have been angry when she left again that night. Yet I wasn't really, or at least not entirely. When she left again with her friend, I was mostly just jealous that she had chosen him. He had taken first place, while her two only daughters had taken second.

Fight or Flight

When the morning came,

I finally took flight,

  just like the racing birds I had spotted when I was younger.

I regret every moment I spent in the sky.

Mostly because I had abandoned my little sister, leaving her to cry.

Second Choice

You told me I was your sunshine.

I suppose his grey clouds could overpower my little light.

Time and time again, you chose his cast of clouds over my little spot
   of sun.

And perhaps that's why all turned gloomy for you.

Swimming Lessons

I learned how to swim.

I was taught the breaststroke and how to float on my back.

I've found peace in the water; I'm able to hold my breath.

Zoe never learned how to swim.

She was thrown straight in the deep end.

Her lungs never received any air.

She was never taught how to float.

All she knows is war in the water.

Moving Day(s)

He left first.

The leaving of my father was like a scrape on a knee.

She left second.

The leaving of my mother was like losing a limb.

Zoe left third, to move in with our father.

The leaving of my little sister was the complete rupture of my heart.

Each moving day, I became emptier than I was before.

And as the years went by, I grew more and more tired.

Please, Life, just let me have a rest.

Delusion

Through the lens of deception, my mother must have viewed her
moving out as an act of bravery.

In her twisted mind, she must have tricked herself into believing
her isolation was an act of courage.

And yet, even the most charming isolation turns into miserable
solitude.

Make-Believe

When I am surrounded by people, I tell myself I am all right.

When I am surrounded by people, I laugh louder than anyone else
   in the room.

When I am surrounded by people, I act like the girl everyone
   expects me to be.

When I am surrounded by people, I play make-believe.

When I am alone, I stop pretending.

When I am alone, I feel fear trembling through my bones.

When I am alone, I cry an ocean of tears.

When I am alone, I don't have to play make-believe.

Do people notice the mask I wear?

The Abused and the Abuser

"I hate you!" she screamed, with all of her might.

Her words were knives in the blue evening.

Her words stabbed into my heart, just as I'm sure they stabbed into
   hers.

I vowed I would never howl such hurtful words back at her,
   at anyone.

Yet, a few months later, I found myself screaming, "I hate you!" with
   all of my might.

My words were daggers in the cold, night air.

I'm sure my words shot straight into her heart, just as they shot
   straight through mine.

Nightmares

I had this terrible dream once, in second grade.

I dreamt that I had woken up, when I had not really.

In this disturbed dream, I ran to my parents' room to climb into their
  bed.

When the blankets covered me, I realized my parents had been
  replaced by monsters.

I screamed in horror in the face of these alien creatures.

Little did I know that nightmare was a foreshadowing of what was to
  come.

1:09 a.m.

My care for you is overwhelming.

It always comes in waves.

The waters are calm and then a massive tidal wave hits.

Suddenly, I'm drowning and don't know how to swim.

Seventeen

Prior to my seventeenth year, I felt extraordinary.

Yet, in the reign of my dancing-queen years, I felt pathetically dull.

In your absence, life began to be less special.

Through tears, you spoke softly,

"I'll always love you. You're still my blue-eyed baby."

When you first held me in your arms,

did you plan on leaving me?

Missing

I believed our love was as constant as the North Star.

The day rose and fell.

And when night came, I couldn't find you anywhere.

Kid Again

I was the child, yet the kid in you was beginning to show.
Not in an adventurous, wonderful way;
There was no wonder in your eyes.
You appeared little.
Every movement timid, every word unsure.
All I wanted to do was find you a cure.

Recliner Chair

"Please tell me," I begged.

I could sense the darkness that danced in the air.

I had felt it for a while now.

With every passing day, the dance turned more violent.

More harsh. More cold.

It was becoming all quite overwhelming.

So there I sat, in the recliner chair, begging to be told what I already knew. Staring into the eyes of my grandparents, just to hear them utter the words I had been expecting this entire time. Yet, I still felt tremendously nervous, unlike any that I had experienced prior.

Nothing else compares to that very moment.

"Just tell me," I urged.

The silence was choking me.

I could feel my lungs shriveling into emptiness.

Second by second, the stillness of the hushed room was taking my life. If a word wasn't spoken soon, my dried-up corpse would certainly have been found in the recliner chair.

Spoken words slowly found their way into the void of the room, and suddenly life took form in me again.

The beating, complete heart in my chest had been replaced with one more broken.

My full lungs were replaced with a pair much more shallow.

I had sat down in the recliner chair a very certain person.
I got up from the recliner chair one very different.

I expected my first heartbreak to be the fault of some doltish boy, not by the wrongdoings of my parents.

How-To

They tell you how to get over a boy.

They tell you, "There are plenty of fish of the sea."

But you aren't a fish to me, you are the ocean in its entirety.

Nobody can replace you.

They don't tell you how to get over your mother.

Heartbreak

When a romantic relationship ends,

I assume it happens suddenly.

There's a moment when the sinking realization of "it's over" settles
  in.

There are possibly some warning signs beforehand.

No more phone calls from their number.

When you reach for them, their touch is cold.

And the heartbreak might last a while,

But there is a quick moment when the heart actually breaks.

When your parents break your heart, there is no moment of
  realization.

There is no foreshadowing.

There are no signs.

They do not gradually stop calling you; they just leave.

They do not tell you why they don't tuck you in at night anymore.

There is no explanation for why they are no longer around.

When your parents break your heart, it is not quick.

It is a lifetime of pain.

Methamphetamine

Like a puzzle, all the pieces fit together.
Except one.

There was a gap in the center of the mystery you had created.
As I read article after article about meth and its uses,
Filling my brain with the facts of your addiction,
I still couldn't understand why.

Why did you do it?

"People do drugs because they don't like how they feel without them."

Don't you remember telling me that, Mum?

Sewing Machine

She had an urgency in her movement, a wicked look in her eyes.

She shouted on the porch and pounded the door.

I didn't want to let her in. I wanted to pretend I wasn't home.

But I pushed away the thoughts of knowing better and let her in
  anyway. How could I turn my own mother away?

It was just us in the house. Me and her.

I should not have been terrified, but I was.

There was no one else around to protect me, no one else to warn or
  stop me.

I was at the edge, following her every move. She yelled at me for
  that, telling me I didn't need to hover around her.

I think, deep down, we both knew otherwise.

Her purpose, she claimed, was to get the vacuum
  to clean her apartment.

But as she moved into the kitchen, she devised another plan.

"Grandma said I could take it," she repeated over and over again.

"She knows I'm coming to get it."

I doubted her, possibly because Susie never mentioned anything
  about this to me or more likely because my trust in my mother had
  been gone for a while now.

Like a child, with a small voice I said, "Wait to get it later, when
  Grandma and Grandpa are back."

She refused, insisting she needed it right then.

Urgency, urgency.

There was always urgency, an inability to wait.

Her words pressed and pressed me, creating a ringing in my ears, an exhaustion in my heart. She had no reasonable explanation; she never did.

But her screams overruled logic. I caved.

She left the house with the vacuum and sewing machine in her dishonest hands.

The sewing machine was found in the pawn shop a few weeks later. Her addiction had been fed.

False Alarms

I try to restore my trust in you.

I swear, with all my might, I want to believe your words are true.

But when I look in your eyes, I see a shadow of doubt,

And I'm reminded of all of the times you cried wolf when nothing
    was there.

Beautiful Lies

The worst part was realizing your beautiful lies all played a role in
  your twisted plot,
Each word fabricated to further your manipulation.
To you, we are only pieces in your sick game of chess.

I think you're supposed to feel love, not fear,

when you look at your mother's face.

And yet, I find myself wincing every time she is near.

Las Vegas

My mum ran away.

My mum ran away.

My mum ran away.

She's gone again.

My mum ran away.

My mum ran away.

Why is it that I can't do anything to make her stay?

My mum ran away.

She chose him over me, again.

Gone again.

My mum ran away.

Last Words

I asked him, "What the last thing you told your mum?"

"In person or over the phone?" he asked.

I responded, "In person."

His answer was what I expected: he loved her and he would see her
soon.

When he didn't return the question to me, I was relieved.

I didn't want to admit I couldn't remember the last thing I told my
mother.

I can't even recall the date I saw her last, much less what my last
words were to her.

The Good Days

What I miss most of all are the ordinary days.

Summer days passed watching television or sharing company
  in silence.

What I didn't realize then was that

Just being with you

Was extraordinary enough.

I took you for granted, I know I did.

And that's what I hate most about myself.

The Mum Who Cried Wolf

The most embarrassing thing about her life is that no one knows if she's lying or not. And she has to live with that.

And so do we.

Broken Glass

The breaking of my heart is like the shattering of glass.
The healing of my heart has been picking up the pieces and placing
them back together.

But when I think I am complete again, there always seems to be a
misplaced, broken piece.
When I reach for that piece, the glass cuts my skin, I bleed, and I am
hurt all over again.

Old Home

I used to hate that house.

I found the zip code and address to be shameful.

I did not realize that, in our old home, our family was at peace more
than it would ever be again.

I did not realize, years later, I would find myself longing to be back
within those walls.

I keep seeing our old home in my dreams.

The flaws of my parents fit me like a glove.

Their faults have become my insecurities.

Akin

In my reflection, I see parts of you staring back at me.

My nose is shaped just like yours; our eyes share the same color.

When my voice rises, I hear echoes of your shouts.

With each mistake I make, I feel closer to you.

I changed myself to be a contrast to you and your errors.

I have worked so hard to be different from you.

Yet, we are akin.

We share the same skin; I cannot change this.

I want to run away to a place where

not even the clouds in the sky

resemble your face.

Locked Doors

"It's funny that you lock the doors even when everyone is home,"
  he says in broad daylight.
The list of stolen items bites at my lips.
I want to reveal everything that went missing.
The wedding rings, vacuum, the sewing machine, laptop, tennis
  racket, gardening tools, Grandpa's telephone...
  and the list continues.
Yet I stay silent.
How could I explain the truth without being ashamed?
There is no room for understanding.
After all, his mum isn't a criminal.

The Ghost of You

You never left me completely.

I cannot fall asleep without you haunting me.

I cannot hear a song without hearing your voice singing along.

I cannot see the color green without remembering it was your
favorite.

I can only feel incomplete in your absence and reflect on past
memories.

September 2, 2017

I miss my mum.

I can't recall the last time I saw her face to face.

I feel so lonely. I can't stop crying, can't stop feeling.

I hate not having her around to tell me my curfew is earlier than I'd like or there to hold me tight when I need her to.

I wish she was still around to tell me I need to spend the night in instead of out.

I miss my mother...

I found two cards that she wrote me tucked in behind a book.

I miss her handwritten words.

I miss seeing her freckles that cover her arms or hearing her laugh, her real laugh.

I miss her more than I could ever imagine. I can't write anymore.

All the love. Yours truly,
Alexandra Rain

October 7, 2017

It's an overwhelming kind of feeling, growing up, I mean.

I don't know if I can put this feeling into words.

It's all very strange.

I saw my first-grade teacher today and it was a weird reminder of the

obvious fact that I was once seven and now I'm seventeen.

It's all so...odd.

I have a bit of a headache trying to piece my life together.

All the love. Yours truly,

Alexandra Rain

Nightmares, again

"The money, just give me the money, give me anything,
  give me the money."

You are chasing me, just like before.

When I try to run, it feels like I am moving in honey.

I can't escape. Suddenly you are three feet ahead of me.

Beating around every corner, breaking through any locked door.

"The money, just give me the money, give me anything."

You scream and scream and scream.

I beg, cry, plead for you to go.

"The money, just give me the money."

Suddenly, we are at the top of the stairs.

You have that wicked look in your eyes, knife in hand.

You smile because we both know how this will end.

"The money."

Incomplete

There was a fullness in my childhood that I don't have now.

When I reflect on my younger years, I feel empty.

Have I really been so weathered by the storm that I can't recognize the face in the mirror?

When my hands meet pen, I am suddenly able to say so much more than I ever could in spoken conversation.

I shouldn't feel like a stranger to my own parents.

My parents shouldn't feel like strangers to me.

Closer to You

With every word I speak, I feel myself shriveling.

My sentences don't stitch together properly.

Dear God, am I becoming my mother?

To-Do

I fill up all my days with task after task,
The mask of being proactive.
Yet, when everything is checked off the list,
There is one thing I can't do:

Be with you.

I would throw away all the productivity if I could have even just a
  minute with you,
One regular minute like how it used to be.

Quitting

I have reached a point beyond exhaustion.

This feeling that sits in my bones is no longer just "tired."

This feeling that plays with my hair is no longer just "confusion."

I am far past frustration.

My limbs feel heavy to my body, my thoughts weigh on my heart.

Dear God, is this giving up?

Only a Matter of Time

"Your mother is going to lose her job."

"Don't say that. It won't happen."

And then it did.

"Your mother is going to move out."

"Don't say that. It won't happen."

And then it did.

"Your mother is going to end up in jail."

"Don't say that. It won't happen."

And then it did.

"It seems our troubles follow us everywhere,"
Grandpa said when Mum called us from jail.

The Role He Plays

I examined the mugshot, wondering how on earth could this
  possibly be my mother.
Right below her photo was his.
Her friend with the wicked eyes, crooked smile, addiction to heroin.
I wondered – if it wasn't for him, would she still have ended up
  there?

Reactions

When you hear your mother is in jail, you should not feel relief.
But I did.
When you hear your daughter is in jail, you should not laugh.
But Grandpa did.
When you hear your mother or daughter or sister is in jail,
  you should cry.
Trust me, we all did.

Him to You and Me

I believe there is good and bad in every human being.

With that friend of yours, I only saw the bad.

I suppose, somehow, despite all that he is, you must have seen
some good.

Right? You would have had to, wouldn't you?

Why else would you let someone drive you out of your daughter's
life?

Why would you steal for his addiction?

Was he the reason you got addicted in the first place?

I mean, you would have had to see some good in him for you to wind
up in jail with him.

Wouldn't you, Mum?

But he isn't good to me.

He's the man who ruined my mum's life.

Silver Screens

We are all playing the role we believe we should.

We speak the lines that were assigned to us.

We go through the motions as if the actions mean anything.

Our lives feel unreal; nothing more than what's on the silver screen.

And when the film is over, and everyone leaves the theater,

   we are left with who we really are.

Empty people with nothing but the consequences of the reality

   we've created.

After Jail

My mother's return was strange.

I wasn't sure how I should act around her.

I didn't say much.

She didn't say much either, most likely because of her exhaustion.

I observed as she lay on the couch.

I listened as she confided in her older sister for the first time in a
   long time.

I guess they both finally considered me old enough to listen to adult
   conversations.

I no longer had to eavesdrop.

My mother talked about her friend, the one she had ended up in jail
   with.

The one who was there when she was late picking me up.

The one who was always around when trouble lurked around the
   corner.

"There's nothing romantic going on," my mother assured her sister.
"We're just friends."

And quite suddenly, or maybe it wasn't suddenly at all, my mother
   began to cry.

I had grown used to seeing her tears and hearing her weep.

It didn't hurt as much as it used to.

No one said anything.

She repeated herself, saying, "We're just friends,"

and,

"I guess it shows you how desperately I need company. I just want someone to understand."

What Once Was

My mind is spotted with conflict, eternally doomed with the
crashing of thunder; thoughts I cannot erase.

Pounding hour after hour, circling around the idea of what you once
were and what has become.

And despite this, I would not erase you for a spotless mind or the
warm filling of the sun.
I would stand through the storm, hour after hour, because there's a
part of me that still remembers when you were good.

Being kind to you is tearing off my own skin to cover your stripped bones.

I used to wear my heart on my sleeve.

I must have tucked it away some time ago,

because I keep choosing fear over love.

Proper Love

Am I capable of simple love?

 Or am I trapped by my twisted roots?

Do I only know love when it is disorganized and complicated?

Rubber Band

I am stretched and elongated, from one end to the other.

With each barbarous pull, the core of my soul is torn.

Conflicted from all ends to be the means of doing "what is right."

"Be more peaceful," they tell me.

"Why can't you get along with your mother?" they ask.

As the pulling continues, so does the war of words.

Like a rubber band, soon I will snap.

A Telephone Call With My Father

"Nobody listens to me!" I cried.

"Nobody? What do you mean nobody?"

"I mean, everybody ignores what I have to say and my feelings."

"You can't include me in that 'everybody.' You don't talk to me. I don't
   know anything about you. You don't talk to me."

I tried to speak but the words wouldn't escape my lips.

Instantly, I saw the previous years zoom by my face.

In each one of them, my father missing.

I had always pushed the blame to his side, but perhaps the fault
   could only be found on mine.

Nightmares, Again and Again

You were the star of my nightmares, the subject of evil.

It's taken months and months of waking up from these horrors to realize you aren't evil, just completely torn and damaged from the cruelty of life.

Life itself has been a nightmare to you.

Learning to love you again is a mountain nearly impossible to climb.

Progress, Eventually

Someday soon, I know I will be able to look at you and not shift
away.

Eventually, I'll hear your voice as it once was before.

With time, I'll find the strength I had when I was younger.

Somewhere Between

I do not hate my mother.

Not entirely.

I want to hate her completely for the chaos she has caused.

I want to scream with all my might until my lungs are empty,
  "Can't you see the disaster you've created? Are you so blind that
  you can't recognize we're all wearing ourselves down in an attempt
  to clean up your mess? Your horrible mess!"

There are plenty of moments when my anger feels so strong, so
  heartbreakingly powerful, I could explode.

But despite my enormous anger, I do not hate my mother.

I can't.

Even after it all, when every ounce in my being yells at me,
  "Hate her! Ignore her! Forget about her!" I find myself unable to.

I don't hate my mother, possibly because there are parts of her I
  cannot forget.

When I look at my mother, I see not only a woman who's entangled
  herself in a web of addiction but a woman of ages past.

In her dull eyes, there is still a dim light, barely visible but I can spot
  it if I really search.

When she speaks, her sentences are disoriented, yet her tone
  resembles that of a woman I once admired.

Her body seems so foreign to me, so distant from the mother who
  used to hug me warmly.

When I wrap my arms around her shriveled body, it feels like a
disease, a deadly coldness, is attaching itself to me.

Her shriveled body, however, casts a shadow of what once was.

I cannot hate my mother entirely because I still remember.

I remember what it's like to have my mother come to my
performances, with a bouquet of flowers in hand.

I remember the joy of waking up on Christmas mornings to see my
mother's sweet face.

And even though she was swimming in debt, I remember she did all
she could to provide us with what we needed and more.

I remember her laughter, how it could fill up an entire room.

I remember climbing into my mother's bed after a nightmare.

I remember my mother's care and pure comfort.

I remember what my mother's love felt like.

I do not love my mother.

Not entirely.

Despite the wonderful woman my mum once was, I have to remind
myself who she is now.

When I look at my mother, I see a woman who ruined her life and
wreaked havoc with those around her.

I see a woman who is so lost in her world of confusion, she cannot
recognize what is right in front of her.

She cannot comprehend the misery in her mother's eyes or the
disappointment in her father's frown.

She does not see the lines of distress on her siblings' foreheads as they plead, again and again, for my mother to seek the help she needs.

Or perhaps she does understand, and that's what moves her away.

My mother's absence makes the distinction of who she was compared to the stranger she is now.

And because of this, my relationship with her exists somewhere between hate and love.

Hide and Seek

Since childhood, a peculiar kind of hollowness has taken form
   in me.
Emptiness has raided my skin and bones,
Left me feeling incomplete.
Yet I am finding old parts of myself,
 Hidden and scattered throughout.
These little treasures remind me of who I once was.
Like a kid again, I find myself playing hide and seek.
And with each find, I am closer to me.

Fall Down Seven, Stand Up Eight

Learning how to forgive is like learning how to walk.

It's continually stumbling and falling,

But somehow finding the courage to stand back up again.

Or at least trying to.

Adaptability

When I tell people about the hardships in my life, I no longer have a
knot in my throat or tears in my eyes.

If I'm lucky, my hands won't shake.

I'm unsure if I should be proud of my adaptability to such a strange
situation.

So much of her pain is accounted to

the need she feels to do "the right thing."

Winston

I was rushing out the door again, finding new ways to distract myself
from the disaster.

The dark figure across the street would have gone unnoticed if he
hadn't cried out, "Have you seen your mother?"

As soon as his voice hit the air, I collapsed back down to reality.

My thoughts darted from one taunt to another.

I was less concerned about how this man knew whose daughter I
was than seized by the thought that he might be the one from the
past, the "friend" who had played a primary role in my mother's
downfall.

My eyes adjusted and my heart calmed.

I had never seen this man before.

I answered quickly.

"No, I haven't."

I got in the car, shifted to reverse, and began leaving the driveway.

I stopped, shifted the car back to park, opened the driver's door, and
yelled, "I could try to get hold of her if you want..."

"Would you? That'd be great."

"Yeah, I can try. I don't really have much contact with her."

A softness brushed over his face, a look I had never seen before.

Normally when I told the truth, people gave me a look that made me
feel less than normal.

"I know. I'm sorry."

"What is your name?"

"Winston."

"Winston, I'll tell her you were here."

I drove away.

I began to cry.

But for once, my tears weren't because I felt sorry for myself or
because I hated the situation I was in.

This short encounter was different from any of those I had
experienced the past few years.

Normally, when people told me they were sorry, they looked at me
as if the events in my life were some terrible disease I was tragically
afflicted with.

They never looked at me or spoke to me in an understanding
manner.

I cried because I felt like someone finally understood.

Only a Matter of Time, Again

"Your mother is going to get kicked out of the apartment, she's going
to be homeless."

"Don't say that, it won't happen."

And then it did.

Goodbye

Thursday night my mother slept over.

When Grandma told me, I began to hyperventilate.

The last time I had a panic attack that bad was when I was ten

   or maybe eleven.

I didn't scream this time, like I did then.

I didn't howl or alarm anyone.

I didn't rip out my hair.

I didn't do anything; I couldn't.

I felt like I couldn't move.

The kitchen floor didn't feel like spikes this time but rather like a

   pile of quicksand I was sinking through, only to quickly become

   nothing at all.

I don't know how long that sensation lasted.

Three minutes, maybe thirteen, maybe twenty.

Maybe only for a second.

It didn't matter.

I had lost all track of time.

I was terrified.

I had never felt more unsafe in my own home.

The thought of being under the same roof as my mother was

   horrific.

I feared my nightmares were becoming a reality.

More realistically, I was worried my mother was going to steal what she could and flee in the middle of the night.

Grandma took the right precautions, however, hiding all the keys and anything of great importance.

The night passed.

Nothing went missing, and my mother was still there in the morning.

I skipped school that day.

I woke up late, and my mother woke up even later.

I avoided her.

I didn't like how I felt around her.

I hated how she could bring out the worst in me in a matter of seconds.

But I could only stay in my room for so long before I decided to go downstairs.

And there she was.

She, and all of her things, sprawled out in the back room.

She had reduced what she owned to the contents of a few bags.

She was going to be homeless.

I tried to avoid that fact.

Hours later, when we were saying our goodbyes, there was no avoiding it.

I watched, and eventually helped, my mother stuff the very last of her things into her new, beat-up car.

It was the worst moment of my entire life.

And yet, it was also one of the best.

For the first time in three years, I could finally see my mother clearly and I felt she could finally see me.

That part was good.

We both cried a lot.

I told her I wished her life had turned out differently.

I told my mother I knew we both deserved so much more.

My mother told me she didn't want me to worry about her.

I think we both knew that would be impossible.

I asked where she was going to go.

She said she didn't know.

I asked if she was going to stay with her old friend.

She said no.

She told me I was the most important thing that had ever happened to her, kept repeating how much she loved me.

She thanked me for being a good sister to Zoe.

I asked if I would see her again.

She asked if I wanted to do anything for my birthday or if I wanted to have a graduation party.

I told her no.

Why would I?

Neither event really felt important in the midst of all that was happening.

I apologized more than once.

I don't know what for, exactly.

It just felt like the right thing to say.

For the first time in three years, my mum apologized too.

She said she was sorry for all of it.

She apologized for not being a good parent, for being a loser.

And she told me she loved me again, more than anything.

I followed her out to her car.

She told me her original plan had been to give this car to me, after
   she got the money that never came.

The car, truthfully, was a piece of junk.

I think we both knew that.

But the quality of the car doesn't matter.

The point is she was still trying to give to me.

Even when she had nothing, she wanted to give me something.

Even when she was seconds from being homeless, she still tried.

And that should count for something.

We cried some more.

We hugged some more.

We said goodbye, over and over.

And then she left.

The Last Time

Mortality has taught me a fine lesson.

Tested me until my bones were weak.

Pressed me time and time again.

Reminding me I will never know when our time will be the last.

When I say goodbye, I repeat "I love you" until the words feel right.

I go back for the third, maybe fourth, hug until I feel my arms wrap
   tight enough.

I let my eyes linger, taking everything in as a whole.

I wish I'd had this knowledge before.

If I had, I would have said "I love you" more firmly.

I would have hugged you until my arms grew weak.

I would have admired the light in your eyes, just a little bit longer,
   embracing you when you were whole.

What Once Was No Longer Remains

There are new people in what was your apartment.

I saw them.

Their car parks where yours once did.

Their bed is now where yours once was.

You're no longer across the street in your small apartment.

You're on the streets now.

I don't know where.

Just Tell Me the Truth

Almost a week after her leaving, I got a message from my mother.

She had a new phone number, again.

We conversed back and forth through text.

I asked her over and over again, "Where are you?"

No response.

Finally, I had the courage to call.

Quite frankly, I was surprised when she answered.

"Where are you?"

She told me she was in Las Vegas.

"Are you staying with your friend?"

No response.

"Mum, are you staying with him?"

I could hear the answer before she even spoke it.

"Just tell me the truth."

She told me she was.

I didn't think it possible, but when she uttered the word "Yes,"

  my heart broke one more time.

An Apology

Mum, I'm sorry.

I'm sorry I didn't spend enough time with you when you were
  around.

I'm sorry I spent all my nights out, instead of inside with you.

I'm sorry I didn't realize how much you needed me, and how much I
  needed you.

I'm sorry I never hugged you tight enough.

I'm sorry I just assumed things were going to get better.

I'm sorry I didn't put in more effort.

I'm sorry I didn't include you in my life when I should have.

I'm sorry I didn't listen to you.

I'm sorry this is the life we got together.

I know we both deserve so much more.

Most of all, I am sorry I do not have the courage to say this
  to your face.

Mum, thank you for giving me life

and allowing me to have these experiences.

One Last Plea

I'm so tired, Mum.

Please just come home.

Growing Pains

My growing was painful.

Growing up was receiving a call from jail in January.

Staining my heart with despair in February.

Feeling horribly out of place in March.

Growing up was watching my mother disappear during April
    showers.

Dreading Mother's Day in May.

Breaking bones in June.

Growing up was being pushed straight into the deep end of the pool
    in mid-July.

Forgiving, but not forgetting, in August.

Becoming dizzy listening to your illusioned version of truth in
    September.

Growing up was unwrapping the actual truth in October.

Staring at the sky, wondering "Where are you, God?" in cold
    November air.

Growing up was the darkest days in December.

And throughout the years, my growing was learning.

It was teaching myself how to forgive those who don't deserve to be
    forgiven, how to love when I felt I had nothing to give.

It was picking myself up off the ground every time I fell or ripping
    off the bandage even when I felt I wasn't ready.

Growing up was putting on a brave face and reminding myself it would work out eventually.

My growing was painful.

Yet those growing pains have shaped me to be the very person I am today.
I would not wish this pain on anyone else, but it is mine, and I would not trade it for the world.

Acknowledgements

First and foremost, thank you to Tiffany Grayson, my editor and mentor. Thank you, Tiff, for guiding and believing in me. Without your help, my story would be unheard. Thank you, Anna Grayson, to the moon and back for sharing your talent and illustrating my words. Thank you, Mike Thomas, for sharing your marketing knowledge. It is because of you that my poetry is able to reach a larger audience. Thank you Suzanne Brady, Ella Olsen, Liz Yokubison, Tim Smith, and Ethan Jones for all of your knowledge and help. Thank you to the many organizations, nonprofits, and centers that are researching and helping those with addiction and mental health disorders. Together, we can make a difference.

Mum and Papi, without you this story could have never been written. Thank you for all you have done for me, and the lessons I continue to learn from you.

Grandma and Grandpa, thank you for being my guardian angels. Thank you for your support through all of these years. I am forever grateful for your encouragement and love. To my brothers, sisters, aunts, and uncles, thank you for being a light in the darkest of times.

Thank you, dear reader, for letting me share this part of myself with you. Thank you for making it to this very page. I will always be grateful for you. Sincerely, and forevermore, thank you.

To my nine-year-old self: you finally wrote your first book.

About the Author

In the year of 2000, I came to be.

Born in a state surrounded by mountains,

But I never learned to ski.

Born with curious eyes,

The only child of six to have the color blue.

Born from a mother and father with different skin,

Prompted people to ask, "Where are you from?

I answer, "My father is from the Dominican Republic, my mother is

from the states, and my grandpa is from England."

In the year of 2018, I was declared an adult,

Prompting people to ask, "Where are you going?"

I answer, "Anywhere my words can bloom."

Alexandra Rain lives in Utah and, at the time of publication, is a

student at the University of Utah. When Alexandra isn't writing,

she enjoys dancing/choreographing, watching independent films,

and painting.

For more information, please visit growingpainsbyrain.com.

Made in the USA
Columbia, SC
03 March 2020

growingpainsbyrain.~~com~~
@ gmail.com.

88683729R00072